NORTH COUNTRY TRADITIONS

PART ONE: JANUARY—JUNE

by

Joan Poulson

To
Gertrude Atkinson
in admiration of her courage and
zest for life

Published by Hendon Publishing Company Limited, Hendon Mill, Nelson, Lancashire.
Text © Joan Poulson, 1977
Printed by Fretwell & Brian Ltd., Howden Hall, Silsden, Keighley, Yorks.

INTRODUCTION

England has changed more radically this century than in any corresponding period and emerged from World War Two irrevocably altered.

Previously, the majority of the population lived closer to the land, with correspondingly numerous beliefs associated with nature. Lives revolved around and into the seasons; traditions of the past were accepted as the norm and the continuance of customs provided a permanent point of reference to background stability.

It is difficult today, in our smooth and pseudo-sophisticated society, to realise how vital the customs of the past were to communities and families alike. They provided the recurrent highlights of otherwise uneventful lives, but lives which nonetheless were satisfying in daily labour and family conviviality. Whereas today many suffer from an excitement-craving syndrome, life a century ago revolved simply and satisfyingly around the seasons. Natural change and rhythm provided a wealth of interest in combination with the ups and downs of daily life encountered in the extended family then considered desirable.

People loved celebration and gathered eagerly to join in processions, to sing and dance or merely act as observers in flag-waving joviality as each season turned or annual event arose. These festivities can be compared with present-day football matches or protest demonstrations, although earlier, where pent-up energy was released in games, dancing and sports, participation generally proved harmless.

Everyone combined to create amusement and pastimes and this involvement was vital in the life of communities which were beguilingly smaller units than government, not society, now demands.

Customs promoted a great sense of community and where villages were virtually self-sufficient, with an expert always available to offer assistance, from farrier and mid-wife to carpenter and clergyman, everyone combined in celebrating such customs to create not only a stable community but a joyfully united festival. Almost lasting from one event to the next, rehearsals occupied a great part of the limited leisure time.

Completely contrary to this we now suffer from lack of communication not only between generations and members of one family but among contemporaries. The radio has replaced conversation at work and television has become the focal point in the home. Mechanisation has meant that in rural areas fewer people are involved in each task and knowledge of methods or activities of the past are no longer handed down orally. Constant searching after the new and more polished method, from first America then Europe, has forced people to neglect their own culture until we have reached a stage where much that was vigorous and vital to our society has been lost, individualism has evaporated and man has become another assembly-line product. Sadly, when attempts have been made to revive traditional events, the vitality is lacking and robust co-operation has become self-conscious formality.

It is sometimes said that period photographs showing the celebrations of customs last century reveal solemn participants, and this because they felt little pleasure in the event; I would suggest that their solemnity was due to a dignified sense of occasion together with embarrassment before the newly-invented camera.

Too little importance is now placed upon a sense of pride and individuality, we are bound as firmly to the machines invented to ease labour as man ever was bound to the land, but certainly in the past a labourer felt a satisfying involvement in his daily work and usually saw the fruits of his labour benefitting the community. Our bland, mechanised and ultra-efficient lives become continually easier and more lifeless, with entertainment ever on top and the desire to be entertained insatiable.

In the seventeenth century it was written "We old men are old chronicles, and when our tongues go there are not clocks to tell only the time present, but large books unclasped; and our speeches, like leaves, turned over and over, discover wonders that are long since past".

An oral interchange of lore is now vitally important before the sources of much valuable information die and their knowledge becomes extinct. Old people have lived through a completely different era; they belong to a culture unchanged for centuries and deserve the patient attention of experts to record their irreplaceable memories.

Until recently the heritage of our immediate past was ignored, but fortunately many people have realised its worth and have devoted themselves to listening to the old and recording their tales of past days.

Moses Heap, born in Lancashire in 1824, wrote near the end of the nineteenth century "Some of the people living in those far-off days were very quaint characters— as well as superstitious, which trait got grafted into the children, for education was almost nil. They lived such lonely lives amongst the hills, scarcely ever going more than five miles from their native village. No wonder the awful tales told in the firelight on a cold winter's night would have its effect on the young ones. Fairies, wizards, witches—'Billy with The Wisp', 'Jack with the Lantern' and 'Jenny Greenteeth'."

Despite the loss of most of our customs and traditions, many remain and it can be surprising to realise how extensive and deeply-rooted these are in mythology. Strange beliefs and traditions prosper in many parts of the north and some will be described within the context of this book. Statements will also be offered from old people remembering certain customs from childhood and these might be found to be particularly valuable in clarifying details of the events.

With reference to my statement on the time spent rehearsing for festive occasions, a woman of Farnworth, in Lancashire, said "We always had a May Queen, who was chosen by vote and we had practices for weeks beforehand." She referred to the years soon after the turn of the century, and of the same period a Thirsk man relates "A blind friend of mine, John Corner, who lived here . . . had a group of young men who started to practise in my uncle's front room about the first week of November. I think they had one night a week up to December when they put in more time. He was a concertina player and the party made up about six people. They started off Christmas Eve locally and also went on Christmas Day to neighbouring Sowerby. Then, after, they had the week doing the rounds of villages for quite a good daily mileage and finished New Year's Day about Thirsk—parts that were missed at Christmas. They broke up after the '14 War.''

It will be seen by any person interested in ancient customs that many of them were centred upon the church, although a great number are pre-Christian in inception. For many years the early church tried to abolish primitive rites, and in the eighth century a Council held at Hainault condemned many popular superstitions. At a similar date, St. Eligius, Bishop of Noyou, preached "I implore you not to observe the sacrilegious customs of the pagans . . . Let no Christian pay regard to the paticular day on which he leaves a house or enters it . . . Let no one do on the calends of January those forbidden, ridiculous, ancient and disreputable things, such as dancing, or keeping open house all night, or getting drunk . . . let no one rest on the day of Jupiter, unless it fall on a saint's day; nor observe the month of May."

In the Council of York, 1466, all superstition was denounced as idolatry.

As time elapsed, the essentially innocent aspect of the ancient beliefs was allowed to percolate the Church's Calendar and the lively, joyful aspect of Christianity began to pervade church festivals.

May ancient cult figures have survived to become innocent characters in folk-lore and pagan gods have become familiar figures of tradition. Thus we obtained characters for the Pace-Egg Play and Mummer's Plays, while the traditionally English May-Queen once reigned as Flora, Roman goddess of flowers.

Hopefully, those of our customs which survive will go from strength to strength and young people will come to respect and admire the traditions of their country, but even at the beginning of the last century there was already a depletion in the number of festivals celebrated annually. In 1820, Washington Irving on a visit to Yorkshire commented "One of the least pleasing effects of modern refinement is the havoc it has made among the hearty old holiday customs. It has completely taken off the sharp touchings and spirited reliefs of these embellishments of life, and has worn down society into a more smooth and polished, but certainly a less characteristic surface . . . The world has become more wordly. There is more dissipation and less of enjoyment. Pleasure has expanded into a broader, but shallower stream; and has forsaken many of those deep and quiet channels where it flowed sweetly through the calm bosom of domestic life. Society has acquired a more enlightened and elegant tone; but it has lost many of its strong local peculiarities, its home-bred feelings, its honest fireside delights".

JANUARY

Tonight it is the New Years night, tomorrow is the day,
And we are come for our right and for our ray,
As we used to in good old King Henry's day.
    Sing, fellows; sing Hagman, heigh!
If you go to the bacon-flitch, cut me a good bit,
Cut, cut and low, beware of your man;
Cut and cut round, beware of your thumb,
That I and my merry men may have some.
    Sing, fellows; sing Hagman, heigh!

This hearty song was commonly sung in Richmond on New Year's Eve, when it was customary to visit the homes of friends. Gifts, or pieces of cake were exchanged and, according to the song, slices of bacon.

A widespread belief in the north of England was that if anyone had pockets without money on New Year's Eve, or allowed the fire in the home to go out that night, they would suffer ill-luck in the forthcoming year. From early times, much of the folk-lore associated with the new year reveals an anxiety to ward off evil and to procure prosperity during that year. A mid-nineteenth century author recorded that, as a boy, he heard the mistress of the house he was visiting warn her servants not to allow anything to be removed from the house on New Year's Day, although as much as they liked could be carried in. He wrote: 'Acting on this order, all ashes, dish-washings, or potato parings, and so forth, were retained in the house till the next day.' This custom can be traced to the days of the Roman Empire. It was to ensure that more would enter the house in the ensuing year than would leave it.

Much importance was placed upon the person first to enter the house in a new year. It has always been customary for a dark-haired man, preferably carrying pieces of both coal and bread, to be first into the home. Bread and coal were symbols of the plentiful supplies of food and fuel hoped for throughout the forthcoming year and this custom survives, with increasing emphasis the further north one goes. A red-haired or fair man was never acceptable, as tradition says that Judas Iscariot was red-haired. In the West Riding of Yorkshire, doors were barred to prevent a woman entering accidentally as the 'first-footer', for this was believed to bring certain bad luck upon the household.

A person entering another's home on New Year's Day would consider it essential to take with them some small gift. This custom originated in days when Saxon families and friends exchanged presents on the year's opening day. In many country districts young girls carried the wassail bowl round to the homes of neighbours. As each person drank from the bowl they were wished a prosperous year by the girls, a traditional rhyme often being chanted.

Twelfth Day's Eve was always held as a festival in rural England, with mummers performing plays, villagers joining in the games and dancing then feasting of some kind enjoyed by all. The Christian holiday lasted for twelve days, with some villages having twelve small fires and one large one lit at some time during the celebrations. This was to represent Christ and His twelve disciples. One fire, representing Judas Iscariot, was always extinguished immediately, the charred sticks being kicked around with vigorous delight.

Many elderly people still remember visits from the mummers on New Year's Day when youths, dressed in old clothes, sometimes in women's clothes or their own garments turned back-to-front, went from house to house in the neighbourhood. Their faces blackened as a primitive disguise, they carried an odd assortment of dusters, brushes and dust-pans. These were the mummers, and when a door was opened to their knock they rushed into the house making a continuous humming sound between closed lips and miming the actions of dusting or sweeping around the room. Then they took the money offered to them and hurried out, still without saying a word. This welcomed visit symbolised the sweeping away of the old to make way for the new and was common all over the north. People in each of the counties included in this book have described their memories of the mummers' visits, some occurring until the start of the First World War. A woman in Wharton recounted an incident involving the mummers which took place early this century. It occured one Friday evening and her parents had gone to play whist with friends in the village. It was bath-night and, as she was youngest at eight years of age, she was the last to take her turn. Her elder brothers and sisters were already in bed as she sat in the bath which had been placed in its usual spot before the fire earlier in the evening. 'It was New Year time and I was well and truly soaked in the bath when in rushed the mummers. Our doors were never locked of course. I grabbed the towel around me but they just carried on and did everything as usual. I couldn't give them any money as I couldn't get out of the bath.'

A woman in her seventies, living near Warrington, related: 'A party of youths would dress up with their faces black, most would dress like women, wear their coats inside-out, sing silly songs, act silly and they would get money.'

A seventy-one year old woman of Marple narrated in 1974: 'When I was a small girl, on New Year's Day the children of the village used to go to a public house. It was called "The Horse Shoe". We wished them a happy New Year and then each of us would be given an apple, an orange and a bright new penny, which in those days went a long way.'

In the same year a Bolton man told me of the period 1910–1915 when: 'As we grew older, we went to Watch Night Service at church after a social in the schoolroom. The choir usually gave the social.'

In Newcastle-on-Tyne I was told: 'First-footing is still a popular custom. As soon as midnight strikes, the first-footers go visiting, to bring luck for the coming year. The first-footer must be a dark man. He is expected to bring a lump of coal and in some villages he gives a little salt. In return he is given drinks with shortbread and Christmas cake.'

7

For almost nine hundred years, the New Year has been welcomed with ceremony in Allendale, where, a few days before New Year's Day, a huge bonfire is erected. This is to be lit in a very unusual way just before midnight on New Year's Eve. On that evening wooden barrels are partially filled with wood shavings. These are ignited and the barrels then carried in procession around the town on the heads of about forty 'Guisers'. These men later throw the barrels onto the bonfire to light it. In many parts of the north, Guisers enact a similar play to that of the Mummers but usually blacken their faces: this in ancient times formed a primitive disguise—hence the name Guisers.

A man from little Hulton who was born in 1898 explained: 'On New Year's Day all the little children went round the shops wishing them a Happy New Year, and they gave you an apple or an orange or some sweets or a little square box with cachous in . . . and they were scented, I still remember.'

Twelfth Night was a very popular day long ago, when the ancient custom of choosing a King and Queen for the evening was continued. This can be traced back

Left: These stalwart pit deputies, photographed outside a colliery in County Durham in 1900, would have been familiar with all the traditional aspects of first-footing. Probably each of them would have taken home a small piece of coal, personally mined, to carry into the house at midnight on New Year's Eve. This was believed to encourage a plentiful supply of fuel in the forthcoming year.

many centuries and is a symbol of the honouring of the Kings who visited the Infant Jesus. A farming couple, or the local squire, would give a supper in their barn which was richly decorated with evergreens and mistletoe. Friends were invited, sometimes farm-hands or other employees, and an enormous plum cake served during the supper. The cake contained both a pea and a bean, but before the cake was cut it was traditional for someone to recite:

> Now, now the mirth comes
> With the cake full of plums,
> When Bean is King of the Sport here.
> Beside, you must know,
> The Pea also
> Must revel as Queen of the Court here.'

A man was expected to find the bean and a woman the pea; they were then honoured as King and Queen for the evening, with the remaining guests participating as servants or courtiers. There was great hilarity as the royal couple commanded their court to perform ridiculous feats and everyone danced to the music of fiddles.

FEBRUARY

February 2nd is Candlemas day, commemorating the presentation of the Infant Christ in the Temple. Henry VIIIth ordained that: 'On Candlemas Daye it shall be declared that the bearynge of candels is done in the memorie of Christe, the spiritual lyghte.' At that time, everyone went to church on Candlemas Day and consecrated candles were carried in procession around the church. Homes were decorated with branches of box, the foliage remaining in place until Easter, when it was replaced by yew.

> In 1571 Thomas Tusser wrote:
> 'At Shrovetide to shroving go thresh the fatte henne
> if blindefilde can kill it then geve it thy menne,
> Maides fritters and pancakes inough see ye make,
> Let shutte have one pancake for company sake.'

Many references in this verse are explained by the customs of Shrovetide, which consists of the last four days before Lent and includes Egg Saturday, Quinquagesima (or Shrove Sunday), Collop Monday and Shrove Tuesday. Long ago, church bells rang on the Tuesday to call people to church where they would confess their sins and be shriven. The word 'Shrove' derives from shrive, ie., to receive confession and grant absolution or forgiveness, A.S. 'scrifan'.

On Collop Monday all collops or pieces of bacon were used up, while on Tuesday all eggs and butter were utilized in pancakes. This emptying the larder of all rich foods was intended as preparation for the Lenten fast, and in wealthy families all food forbidden on fast days was consumed in enormous meals. Often, Shrovetide was used as yet another excuse for a feast, as very many of the foods found in most homes could be used on fast days.

On Collop Monday it was customary for children to call on friends and neighbours to ask: 'Pray dame, a collop, or we'll give you a whallop' and to be given pieces of home-cured bacon. Later the custom was extended to local shops where a shop-keeper would have tiny bags of sweets ready to dole out to children as they called on their way to school with their plea. Going colloping usually ended at noon but it was the custom at a mill yard in Huddersfield for the owners to give money which was thrown as pennies to the crowd of waiting half-timers. The custom was last observed in 1925.

Right: A photograph taken after the service for the Blessing of the Salmon Nets at the Pedwell Fishery, Norham, near Berwick-on-Tweed. The vicar conducts the service from a coble (small boat) moored by the beach and the congregation of fishermen and sightseers join in the old prayer:
> *Good Lord, lead us,*
> *Good Lord, speed us,*
> *From all perils protect us,*
> *From the darkness us direct*
> *Finest nights to land our fish*
> *Sound and big to fill our wish.*
> *God keep our nets from snag and break,*
> *For every man a goodly take,*
> *Lord grant us.*
The first boat of the season is launched at midnight, February 14th, and if the first shot (net) contains a salmon it is traditionally handed to the vicar.

Shrove Tuesday was, after Christmas Day, the most popular feast day during the mediaeval period and a time for great revels. After the Reformation, although many Shrovetide customs were still popular, pancakes became the dish most closely connected with the season and the ringing of a town's bell was signal for the making of pancakes, for children to be released from school, apprentices from work and the start of vigorous, often violent games of football. The tradition of ringing the Pancake Bell is maintained at Scarborough and Shrovetide Football continued at Alnwick. At Sedgefield, County Durham, the Pancake Bell is rung at noon, then the traditional game of Shrovetide football begins at one o'clock. Initially, the games of football started in the churchyards and were continued throughout the streets, but after years of broken windows and violence many places prohibited the game or had it removed to a place outside the town. At Bromfield the goal was the house of each captain, but in Alnwick the game is played just outside the town with goals four hundred and forty yards apart and around one hundred and fifty on each team.

Shrovetide often became a period when people indulged in a final 'fling' before the restrictions of Lent, and games and sports of all kinds, wrestling, football, and so on occurred all over the country. Football was not always accepted agreeably in England, no doubt due to influence of the Shrovetide games; Edward I referred to football as a 'useless and idle sport'.

In 1975, a seventy-four year old woman of Aspatria told me 'Shrove Tuesday was Pancake Day and we made them with a handful of clean, soft snow in the batter if possible. Mother always said this made them light. We used to go to the town to watch the Uppies and Downies. This was men kicking a ball from one end of the town to the other, sometimes they were all in the river together, it was great fun as long as you stood well back. If the lookers-on got too near the water, they got pushed in. The Uppies had to get the ball from Workington Hall down to the harbour and the Downies had to try and get it up the town to the Hall. Sometimes one of them might get the ball unseen into his jacket or under it and run as hard as he could. Sometimes a shop window or two got cracked.'

An elderly Cheshire man related: 'Shrove Tuesday was a half-day holiday for apprentices and schoolchildren. We used to sing "Pancake Tuesday is a very happy day, if you don't give us a holiday we'll all run away".' This phrase was common everywhere in the north until fairly recently, even well into the period when no holiday was given or expected. The same man told me that his parents referred to the bell rung on Shrove Tuesday as the 'Guttit Bell'.

A Colne woman in her late sixties told me that her brother and his friends, all apprentices, were always given a holiday on Shrove Tuesday when she was a child. 'They spent it marlicking about and playing tricks', she said.

Shrove Tuesday was a day for claiming gifts, and all children—with many adults—traversed the parish, visiting homes to sing and chant a rhyme in return for a 'shroving gift'. This was sometimes known as Lent-crocking and the appeal was often forcibly applied with long banging on the doors. Although Lent-crocking died out in the nineteenth century, many elderly people in the north have described to me how children visited relatives and friends on the morning of Shrove Tuesday asking: 'Please, a pancake.' They were usually given an orange or a few sweets, symbolic of the gifts of pancakes or fat in which to cook one which would have been given a century earlier.

The origin of pancake-making on Shrove Tuesday is obscure, but one theory points to the fact that pancakes were included in the pre-Lenten feasts of the early Greek church, suggesting that the custom became adopted, but in different form, in England. However, it is equally likely that the custom arose simply because pancakes were a convenient way of using bacon fat and eggs.

In North Lancashire, people have described the 'Pancake Parties' which were held until the 1940's. At these, each person had to finish eating their pancake before the next was ready. If they failed they were dumped into a wheel-barrow, pushed to the midden or ash-pit and threatened with being tipped in—much to the enjoyment of the other guests. Young men were deliberately delayed in their pancake-eating by friends. One tactic being to try to snip a pancake from someone's fork with scissors.

Until the end of the last century, it was customary in Yorkshire and other parts of the north for anyone not finishing his pancake before the cook was ready with another to be 'stanged' or drummed noisily from the table. Not ending here, the fun continued with the victim being seized, carried outside and dropped into the midden, providing a great source of laughter and joking for everyone watching.

In most northern localities, mistletoe, holly and other Christmas evergreens were kept until Shrove Tuesday to be used as fuel for the fire on which the pancakes were cooked. I have talked with many elderly people in various northern towns who remember their mothers continuing the custom. Women in Newton-le-Willows (Lancashire), Beverley, Burnley, Barrow-in-Furness, Keswick and Newcastle-on-Tyne are among those who have recounted their memories of the occasion. Men too have been able to describe their part in this Shrovetide custom, their impressions being firmly concentrated upon the fire itself, (especially when they were privileged to put on the twigs), or the pancakes they relished afterwards. For many years it was considered unlucky not to have pancakes on Shrove Tuesday but the custom is no longer given any religious connotation.

At Clitheroe the Town Council met on Shrove Tuesday in the Moot Hall to receive rents, then at 11.30 a.m. the Serjeant at Mace rang the bell of the Hall to inform the townspeople that the Council was ready to begin the annual Boundary Walk. This took place over a period of about five hundred years, beginning in the early fourteenth century when the town's boundary was set and Mear-stones places as boundary markers. It was the responsibility of the Council to walk around the boundary, or Perambulate the Borough, each year. The purpose was to check that no Mear-stones had been moved, as this might cause the town to lose land. The bell-ringing also acted as sign for the boys of Clitheroe Grammar School to 'come out', having spent the morning involved in cock-fighting at school. This Perambulating the Borough or Beating the Bounds is continued in some localities but usually in the latter part of the year.

St. Valentine's Day, still celebrated with anonymous gifts and cards on February 14th, is dedicated both to Valentine, a martyred bishop of Terni and the martyr Valentine whose feast day this is and who had a church dedicated to him on the Flaminian Way in Rome during the fourth century. Neither saint has any apparent connection with either the custom of choosing a partner and sending to him a 'Valentine' card or gift, or the older one of leaving a gift on the doorstep of a friend. The latter custom was common practise in some parts of England within living memory. Perhaps these simple rites derive from the old legend that birds began to select their mates on February 14th, or there may be an older, pagan derivation.

It was apparently customary long ago for children to go singing outside the homes of neighbours on St. Valentine's Day, rather in the way that carol-singing is still practised. An entry in Parson Woodforde's diary on February 14th 1777 reads: 'To 36 children being Valentines Day and which is customary in these parts this day gave £0 s3 0d, being one penny to each of them'.

In the Border Country and Northumberland, young people used to gather together on St. Valentine's Eve to play games. These were all connected with divination, as it was hoped that the name of a future husband or wife would be foretold. One popular method was for the names of all the friends of those assembled to be written upon scraps of paper; these to be put into two bags, boys in one and girls in the other. All present drew a name from the bag containing those of the opposite sex. Three papers in all were withdrawn and if the same name was taken out each time it was certainly expected to be the name of the future partner.

At Norham-on-Tweed, the ancient ceremony of Blessing the Salmon nets is held shortly before midnight on February 14th, when fishermen gather for the short open-air service which no doubt replaces a more ancient rite. The vicar pronounces his blessing just before midnight, so that the first boat of the season can be launched as the clock strikes.

Right: The Kendal Horse Fair photographed earlier this century. A deputation of farmers called upon the Mayor of Kendal in 1851 to discuss the holding of a horse fair to be known as the New Horse Fair. This was sanctioned and held for the first time time on February 22nd, 1852, to be continued annually.

THE HORSE FAIR - KENDAL

The old names for the six Sundays of Lent used to be remembered by the jingle: Tid, Mid, Misere,

Carlin, Palm, Pace-Egg Day.

The first three words are said by some experts to be taken from the psalms appropriate to each particular Sunday, other opinions are that the words come from parts of the Liturgy, particularly the Te Deum. Lent lasts from Ash Wednesday to Easter and includes Mothering Sunday, Carling Sunday, Palm Sunday, Maundy Thursday and Good Friday. Most Lenten customs were subdued, particularly any associated with Ash Wednesday, Maundy and Good Friday. These were generally based upon the religious connection of each day. Lent is traditionally a time of fasting, both to remember Our Lord's fasting for forty days and forty nights in the wilderness and as a personal discipline, self-imposed and unobtrusive. Centuries ago, the fasting was rigid, with fish being the main food of the poor when they could afford it and cheese otherwise. Fritters, figs and vegetables were also recommended as being suitable foods for fast-days but old cookery books reveal that, for many, the fast was often one in name only. Many prescribed dishes were as nutritious and attractive as any, certainly eaten in equal quantity, but of course could only be purchased by moderately wealthy families.

On Ash Wednesday, the clergy burned palms or palm crosses, using the ashes to mark a cross upon the forehead of each member of the congregation. This was to signify that they 'came from ashes and would return to them'. The palms which were used were those which had been blessed on Palm Sunday the year before. Another name commonly accorded to this Wednesday was Fritter Wednesday, because of the custom of eating fritters on this day. In her book 'The Art of Cookery Made Plain and Easy', the 18th century cookery writer Hannah Glasse listed twelve recipes for fritters in a chapter headed 'For a Fast-Dinner, a Number of good Dishes, which you may make use of for a Table at any other Time.'

Mothering Sunday was also given the titles Simnel Sunday, Braggot Sunday and Refreshment Sunday according to the area and was the day in mid-Lent when games were permitted. It was a day when men and women working in remote farms and hamlets, who normally worshipped in tiny 'chapels of ease', returned to their mother church or parish church to share in worship with others of their family. Since many would not normally visit home often during the year, being tied to their jobs as farm labourers or kitchen maids etc., the occasion was marked as important for the family by the baking of a special cake—a Simnel cake, and the children working away from home might gather flowers as they walked the miles to give to their mothers as a token of their love. The family would go together to church then share in a meal, talk and play games in the afternoon before it was time for the workers to depart for their places of employ.

At Altcar, Leigh, Bury and many other towns, a drink of sweetened spiced ale called Braggot was drunk, giving its name to this day.

Old people in Cheshire and Lancashire have described to me how they remember all the family returning to their parent's home on Mothering Sunday. One man in Holcombe told me: 'Everybody went to the mother church for the service then to their parents for tea, but they all took their own food if the family was poor.' He was describing events in the first decade of this century.

An eighty-two year old from Little Hulton told me in 1974: 'It was called Simnel Sunday when you could buy a Simnel Cake in the shops. That was followed by Calf-tail Monday when they stuck a tail on you if you wasn't careful. I was a foreman in a textile mill and I got one stuck on me one Monday. They stuck them on you where the tail should be real. You can just imagine the fun they had at your expense when you was walking about the weaving shed.'

In Bury, streets were crowded every Simnel Sunday in the nineteenth century when confectioners competed to make the finest cakes.

A sixty-nine year old Bolton woman told me in 1975: 'We just knew that (day) as Simnel Sunday and always had a Simnel Cake, a spicy sort of fruit cake, not so rich as Christmas Cake. I was quite big before I realised that Simnel Sunday was also Mothering Sunday. When we knew, we used to get mother a little bunch of violets.' The name Simnel derives from the Latin 'simila' meaning fine flour.

Refreshment Sunday was a name conferred because of the appointed Scriptural reading in churches on this day day of the miraculous feeding of five thousand people from a handful of loaves and fishes.

Since the Second World War the festival has been impoverished and is increasingly given the American name 'Mother's Day'. This was a day created by an American in order that everyone might use the day to show their affection in some special way towards their mothers and has no connection with the traditional Mothering Sunday.

Carling, or Care, Sunday is a name which was commonly given to the fifth Sunday in Lent all over the north of England where it was traditional to eat figs, perhaps cooked in pies or puddings, with dried peas in some cooked form also served during the day. One theory to explain the name given this day is that Care associations with sadness and the origin of Lent. It is said to refer to the inevitable mourning of Good Friday and was given this meaning by Chaucer in 1386 when in his work 'The Clerk's Tale' he wrote: 'Let hym care and wepe'. Within the church this day is termed Passion Sunday.

The dried peas served on Carling Sunday would be soaked overnight and eaten boiled, as a Pease Pudding, with salt and vinegar or even with sugar and rum. They were known as carlin's and this name survives in many parts of the north.

MARCH

Palm Sunday marks the beginning of Holy Week and

the anniversary of Christ's entry into Jerusalem. On this joyful occasion, palms were strewn along His way and this led to the custom, which lasted for many centuries, of people proceeding to church carrying willow branches which they scattered along the lanes as they walked. In rural areas, the willow was often gathered as the villagers passed and tossed down as they continued along their way. The silvery 'pussy willow' has been known as palm for many years and it is still customary for children in some country districts to go 'a-palming' on the day preceding Palm Sunday. Many elderly people in the Warrington area enjoy their memories of times when their children gathered palm for them on this day. These children in turn send, or take, their own families out for palm before Palm Sunday.

Palm Sunday was often known as Fig Sunday, perhaps because the parable of the barren fig tree was read annually in churches on Palm Sunday. It was customary to eat figs, or a fig pudding, as part of the main meal on this day until well into this century. Gifts of figs were given to children and many traditional dishes evolved to be served on the day. It was also referred to as Spanish Sunday, for children carried around bottles of water with pieces of cut-up black Spanish sweet-meat dropped into them. The resulting drink was found to be very palatable by those large groups of children who met on Palm Sunday expressly to walk to a local well or spring where they would fill their bottles with water and ask for a wish to be granted. This custom had no connection with any religious festival although the well would be selected because of some association with a local religious event and be endowed with qualities of holiness. A primitive belief was that water pixies lived inside all wells, but Christianity helped to remove many pagan superstitions. Eventually, religious ceremonies were held beside valuable local wells each year and God's blessing was asked for the source of the water. In many areas though, the wells were thought for centuries to be endowed with special properties, especially those of healing. Services were held to praise God and these wells became known as 'holy' wells. Well-dressing became part of a Christian ceremony: until the end of the 18th century, Cheshire wells were dressed and contemporary writings refer particularly to Mow Cop. Instances of other customs centred upon wells occurred at other times of the year and all over the north; in Nantwich, where the wealth of the town depended upon salt, the brine springs

Right: Two interesting photographs taken at Summerseat in 1970, showing the Bury Pace Eggers in scenes from their traditional play. The fundamental theme of the Pace Egg Play is identical to that of Mummers' plays and Plough Monday plays, as well as the Soul-Cake plays of Cheshire. This theme is of death, with resurrection following, the rebirth of nature, a propitiation of the gods of fertility. In parts of Yorkshire and Lancashire, where the ancient, symbolic drama takes the form known as a Pace Egg Play, the rite is a Spring-time one with the pace egg being a 'pasch' or Easter egg.

were blessed during a ceremony on Ascension Day; on May 1st a 'Waking the Wells' custom was observed at the Eden Lacy caves when bottles of water containing broken pieces of Spanish sticks were shaken beside the well. These 'well-wakings' were celebrated all over the north until this century, but there were local variations. At Gosforth, wine was poured into the well and caught, greatly diluted, through the spout.

Maundy Thursday, the Thursday of Holy Week, was also known in the past as Shere Thursday from the ancient custom of shearing, or cutting, the hair and beard on this day. The name Maunday is derived from the Latin 'mandatum' (command) and one school of thought is that this is connected with Christ's command for all men to love one another. (The Golden Rule of the Christian faith is said to be Matthew 7, verse 12: 'Always treat others as you would like them to treat you'). Other experts say that the name derives from Christ's command to imitate His humility, shown when He washed the feet of His disciples. In the Middle Ages it was customary for the ruler of the country to wash the feet of the poor on this day, giving them money and other gifts. It was also a custom in the church from an early date for priests and monks to wash the feet of twelve poor men. Twelve being chosen as a symbol of Our Lord's disciples. The rite is recorded as early as the seventh century when monks held a simple ceremony to show their humility. In Durham, all the monks knelt in the Cloister Walk to wash and then dry the feet of children. They then kissed the feet and gave gifts to the children. These gifts usually consisted of bread or wafer-cakes in the earliest times, with sometimes red herrings given instead, but in later years money replaced these tokens.

As years passed, the custom was also celebrated by the King and Court. Then the symbolic twelve people became a number equal to the years of the Sovereign's age. When Edward III was fifty years old he washed the feet of fifty poor people, giving each one a gift of a pair of slippers.

By the time of Elizabeth I a gift of twenty shillings was given instead of other objects, and from then on money was to replace any other kind of 'maund' (gift).

James II was the last English king to celebrate the complete tradition and it is recorded that on Maundy Thursday, April 16th 1685 he 'wash'd, wip'd and kiss'd the feet of 52 poor men with wonderful humility'. The event gradually declined and feet-washing was discontinued around 1730. Gifts were given by proxy on the King's behalf but the ceremony was revived in 1932 by King George V.

Right: A photograph taken at Todmorden in 1976, of the Midgeley Pace Eggers. This is a revived group consisting entirely of schoolboys, who perform the ancient play with vigour and enthusiasm. They can be seen at various towns in the Calder Valley during the Easter period.

Maundy coins are now minted specially for the annual ceremony although they are still coins of the realm and one is still given for each year of the Queen's life. The ceremony usually begins at 11 a.m., lasting an hour, and is very colourful with one Lord High Almoner and his assistants being girded with linen towels and carrying nose-gays of sweet herbs as in days of old.

Good Friday, the most solemn day of the church's year is the anniversary of the day when Jesus was crucified. In the Bible we find the words 'he humbled himself, and in obedience accepted even death—death on a cross.

Far right: A huge crowd in Avenham Park, Preston, on Easter Monday 1905, gathered to roll pace-eggs down the hill in traditional fashion. Eggs have been associated with Spring-time for thousands of years and since Christian times have been symbolic of the rock tomb from which Christ emerged after His Resurrection. The custom of exchanging gifts of eggs at Easter developed in England following influence from countries in northern Europe. Games of egg-rolling, egg-dumping or egg-pecking were popular in Germany, France and Austria; other forms of the games were practised among Christians in Asian countries.

In the Middle Ages it was customary to give eggs to one's servants and King Edward I is reputed to have given 450 eggs to members of his household in 1307. The eggs were hard-boiled and richly coloured, with some decoration applied in gilt.

Therefore God raised him to the heights and bestowed on him the name above all names, that at the name of Jesus every knee should bow'. (Philippians 2, verses 8-10.) One authority suggests that the name is a corruption of God's Friday and some European countries refer to it as Holy Friday or Great Friday. The latter name is the one by which is is known in Denmark—Langfredag, a name which can also be translated as Long Friday and in some places it was for centuries referred to as Long Rope Day. In these districts it was customary, usually among fishing families, to take ropes to the foreshore where the entire community would join in skipping games. Scarborough is one town to continue this tradition but it occurs there on Shrove Tuesday when the Skipping Festival is enjoyed by people of all ages on the foreshore.

On Good Friday, most country people in the past refused to work—either from respect, or superstition that to work on this day would bring ill-luck. No blacksmith would ever work with nails because of the appalling purpose for which they were used on the first Good Friday. In the Isle of Man, iron tools would never be used in the home for the same reason and even pokers were put aside and sticks used instead.

In the North Riding of Yorkshire it was generally accepted that the earth must not be disturbed at all and any planting or ploughing activities left until next day. People in some parts of the country, however, held the belief that anything planted on Good Friday would produce an excellent crop, for Good Friday is a day when the earth is completely good and holy since the power

Easter Monday Avenham Park

of Satan is vanquished by the death of Jesus Christ. It was a commonly-held belief in country areas that eggs laid on Good Friday had the power to extinguish fire, while the making of bread or buns was almost certain to ensure good luck throughout the coming year, for if kept, a piece from such a bun would protect the house from fire and bring good fortune to the home. Buns baked on Good Friday were believed to have great curative powers and crumbs from one would be used through the year in home remedies. A belief was also held in the north that if a hot-cross bun was taken to church before the service on Good Friday morning and two friends broke it into halves across the cross saying

'Half for you and half for me,
Between us two good will shall be. Amen'.

Then they would never quarrel as long as each one retained his half of the bun. It is still traditional all over the country to eat hot-cross buns on Good Friday and a theory is that the cross on them is pre-Christian in origin, as bread was so marked in pagan times. This belief is backed by the fact that during the excavations of Herculaneum, a city destroyed in A.D. 79 by volcanic activity, two loaves marked with crosses were found. But since many Roman citizens accepted the Christian faith in the first century it is quite possible that there were Christians then living in Herculaneum who would use the bread in celebration of the Last Supper.

In the nineteenth century it was common to see sellers of 'Hot Cross Buns' on the streets each Maundy Thursday, giving housewives warning of their arrival with their familiar call and perhaps the ringing of a hand-bell.

In some northern regions Good Friday was known as Care Friday, a day of sorrow, when the mountain ash tree was cut and carried into the house to protect it from witchcraft. This pagan custom was prevalent in many countries and the tree, also known as the Care Tree, was believed to have great protective powers against witches who regarded this day as an important one on which to meet.

Children in Liverpool used to blacken their faces and parade around the streets on Good Friday morning until the end of the last century, carrying the effigy of a man. They called out 'Judas! Judas!' as they went, finally throwing the figure onto a fire.

An important Easter custom is the Pace-Egg or Mummers Play, an extension of the ancient mimes perpetuated in the Sword Dance of the north. Similar to the Soul-Cake Play of Cheshire, performed later in the year, Pace-Egg Plays are still enacted in some parts of the country. The story basically contains the elements of good versus evil, or of resurrection after death. There are many local variations, but the principal hero is either St. George, the Prince or the King. The Turkish Knight is usually the villain, other characters being the Doctor, Captain Slasher and, with the Pace-Egg Play, a comic figure, Toss Pot. The Brighouse Pace Egg was revived in 1950 and is performed on Easter Saturday morning; another is enacted in towns of the Upper Calder Valley on Good Friday morning. An early record of a mummers' play was made in the fifteenth century, and during Tudor times the plays were a feature of Court entertainment.

Many people have passed on to me their recollections of pace-egging, for children also involved themselves in the custom by visiting houses in the neighbourhood where they would be given gifts. Local variations abound, but a seventy-six year old Manchester man told me in 1974 that it was a regular custom for schoolchildren to go pace-egging on Good Friday before nineteen-ten (1910) and that afterwards it may have been persisted for a year or two in some localities. The nineteen-fourteen/eighteen war certainly put an end to it. Children used to call door to door, sometimes selected houses in the district where they lived and stated that they were pace-egging. The householder would then offer an egg as a gift.

A seventy-seven year old Preston man related in 1973: 'Pace-egging was when I was a boy in Radcliffe about 1903. I remember the words "The first to step in is Lord Nelson you see, with a bunch of blue ribbon tied under his knee. With a star on his breast like silver does shine, I hope you'll remember next pace-egging time. Whack fol the diddle addy dum, Whack fol the diddle addy dum".'

In 1974 a Bolton man narrated: 'I'm now eighty years old but I remember when I was a boy a gang of us used to black our faces and turn our jackets inside out and visit the local pubs. We used to ask the pub-keeper did they want any pace-eggers and we used to give them a song or two, then moved off to the next pub. If we got threepence each a night singing we did very well. I think it happened around Easter.'

The activity was not confined to boys for several women have described their participation in the event. The blackening of faces was in general a masculine choice but there were exceptions and in 1975 a West-houghton woman, aged eighty-one, told me: 'My late husband's mother was full of old sayings. She used to tell us about going as a child at Easter Monday, blackening their faces with soot, knocking on doors and saying "pace-egg, Missus?" They used to get an egg'.

A Manchester woman told me in 1974 that her father went pace-egging as a boy. She explained: 'I'm eighty, but I remember my old dad talking about pace-egging. I don't know if they all went pace-egging but there were six brothers and four sisters. He used to sing some of the words to me:

"We're four jolly lads, out on the spree
We've come a pace-egging and hope you'll agree,
The first that comes in is th'owd Toss Pot you see
He's a gallant owd lad, in every degree.
He's a gallant owd lad and wears a pigtail,
And all his delight is in drinking mould ale".'

The 'Jolly Boys' performed a Pace-Egg Play in Langdale until 1936, with the characters of King George, Lord Nelson, Old Toss Pot, Jolly Jack Tar, Moll Brown Bags and Doctor John Brown dressed in old clothes and having blackened faces. They visited all the local farms and village houses during Holy Week and were rewarded for their performance with either eggs or money. The opening song began

'There's two or three Jolly Boys all in one mind,
They've come a Pasche Egging and hope you'll prove kind,
With your eggs and strong beer, we make it quite clear,
We'll come no more nigh you until the next year'.

Toss Pot was the first character to sing alone and his words were identical to the last four lines quoted to me by the Mancunian woman in 1974. In the Langdale 'Pasche Egging Song' the Doctor claims that he can cure

'Ipsy, pipsy, palsy and gout,
A plague within, or a plague without.
If there's nineteen devils in this man,
I'm sure to turn twenty out'.

These words as well as many others in the play, are identical to ones in Pace-Egg Plays of many counties of England.

Old people in all parts of the north have reminisced to me about their childhood days and a verse remembered by some in Yorkshire and Cheshire to use at pace-egging time is:

'Pray dame, a Pace Egg,
If you'll give us none,
Your cock'll stand a-straddle leg,
And your hen'll lay a stone'.

The words 'pace-egg' are still used by elderly people to describe their Easter gifts, although when writing, the phrase becomes 'pasche-egg' or 'pache-egg'. This can be directly linked with 'paschal' derived from the Hebrew 'pesach' meaning Passover. The French word for Easter is 'Pacques' and the Swedish is 'Pask'. This oldest festival of the Christian church was observed on different days in the early church. By some at the time of the Jewish Passover, which historically fixes the time of Christs Crucifixion and Resurrection, but observed by others on the following Sunday since this was the day on which the risen Lord was seen. In 325 A.D. the Council of Nicaea met to fix Easter Day as the Sunday after the first full moon following the Vernal Equinox (March 21st.). If the full moon occured upon a Sunday then Easter Day would be celebrated on the next one. In this way, Easter Sunday was fixed between March 22nd and April 25th, depending upon the Spring Moon.

Morris dancing is also closely associated with Easter celebrations but these vigorous dances vary in different regions. In ancient times, the dances formed part of a fertility ritual connected with the coming of Spring and renewal of life. The death and resurrection theme survives in Pace-Egg Plays. Morris dancing was also a part of Whitsuntide celebrations and Shakespeare wrote in Henry V (Act II, Scene 4):

'And let us do it with no show of fear;
No, with no more than if we heard that England
Were busied with a Whitsun morris-dance'.

Lancashire Morris dancing became part of the Rush-bearing ceremonies and annual Wakes celebrations which occurred in late July or August and when the festivities were over, the teams were disbanded for a year. The origin of Morris dancing is unknown but is probably connected with pagan rites to promote crop fertility or to banish evil spirits from the land. The name Morris is sometimes thought to derive from Moorish, a reference to days when all dancers blackened their faces and this was said to be imitative of the dark skins of the Moors from whom the dances were thought to have originated. The face blackening was, however, quite a common practice in pagan times to hide the identity of people involved in any ritual; probably using the word Moorish in connection with the dance was simply to refer to its pagan origin. Some experts claim that the dances arrived with Moorish sailors who settled in Cornwall centuries ago and when mines were opened in the north in the eighteenth century, Cornish-men are believed to have moved there to work, bringing the tradition of their dances with them. This is almost certainly the origin of the distinctive Coconut dances. It is said that two Cornishmen went to Whitworth Quarry, near Bacup, helping to found a group there. The Coconut Dances are peculiar to this area, men with blackened faces wearing red and white kilts, clogs, white stockings and turbans decorated with coloured feathers performing the ancient and unique rite. The dancers tap out a rhythm on wooden discs attached to their hands, waists and knees. The first group formed in the area was at Stacksteads in 1857, then in 1903 the Lee Mill Dancers moved to Britannia to establish there the renowned Britannia Coconut Dancers.

The Furness Morris Men dance Cotswold Morris chiefly and combine it with some sword dancing. At Easter the group tour the area with a Pace-Egg play. The dancers wear white, with flower bedecked hats symbolic of the fertility of nature. As with most groups, sticks are clashed, bells jingled, hands clapped and occasional yells emitted, all part of ancient ritual designed to drive away evil spirits. The dancers in some groups carry white or coloured cloths which they use to perform elaborate movements but frequently drape across the ground. This symbolises the primitive worship of gods of nature and fertility, with a desire to be close to the earth and to propitiate these gods.

The Colne Morris Men are a revived group who perform their colourful dance at Eastertime, beating out the rhythm with sticks in the age-old way. Another well-known and popular group is the Bury Pace-Eggers, who are particularly keen on retaining the characteristics of Lancashire Morris. A group of dancers also flourishes in Manley, many in the Manchester area, also in many other northern towns and villages. Sword dancing has its origins closely woven with those of Morris dancing and the Mummers' Plays but is confined almost entirely to the North of England, usually being performed at Christmastime. Among the most well known teams are the Grenoside Sword Team and the Handsworth Sword Team, both from the Sheffield area, and the Royal

Earsdon Sword Dancers, probably Northumberland's most famous team. Sir Walter Scott encouraged the theory that Sword dances were survivals of Nordic war dances, but many areas of Europe completely unaffected by any Nordic influence, had strong traditions of sword dancing. There are evidences of its being performed in Germany as early as the first century and it is likely that the dance percolated across Europe, being introduced into England by the Danes. This Danish derivation would explain the reason for the dances being found mainly in the north of England; certainly the origins of sword dances are primitive and connected with the struggle for survival between the old year and the new.

In pagan times the hare and sometimes the rabbit were symbols of fertility and new life in Spring. The hare has always been given mystic associations and for centuries the rabbit has been credited with being the donor of Easter eggs to children in many parts of Europe. Known as the Easter Bunny, his first written recognition appears to be in a sixteenth century German book which states: 'Do not worry if the bunny escapes you; should we miss his eggs, then we shall cook the nest'. Also from Germany came a printed story in the seventeenth century describing how the Easter Bunny laid eggs as gifts then hid them in one's garden. This belief is still encouraged in country areas, where Easter Bunny is said to lay eggs of different colours during the week before Easter Sunday. Sweetmeats in the shape of hares or rabbits have been traditional for over a hundred years in Europe and are increasingly made in this country to be sold as gifts along with Easter Eggs.

Easter is the most joyful time of year in the life of a Christian for it was on Easter Sunday that Christ triumphed over death and proved the glorious certainty of His words 'I am the resurrection and the life; he who believes in me, though he die, yet shall he live, and whoever lives and believes in me shall never die'.

Springtime has been associated with rebirth for thousands of years and many Easter traditions are connected with eggs, ancient symbol of life. Over two thousand years ago eggs were presented as a symbol of Spring in China and was later adopted by the Persians, Greeks and Romans. Pagan people heralded the Spring with a great feast to mark the end of Winter, exchanging gifts and lighting bonfires in celebration. Eggs became beautifully decorated, and until recently it was customary for mothers to colour eggs for breakfast on Easter Sunday. A Warrington woman described to me how her aunts each specialised in a particular colour, so that when nephews and nieces went for their pace-egg they ended with a basket of different coloured eggs. 'We had them on Easter Sunday morning, but always fried not boiled because we saved the shells and the colour would have come off in the water. Also the glamour.' A Farnworth woman said of her childhood in the first decade of this century: 'On Easter Sunday we had eggs for breakfast. Lots of people dyed them but we used to have funny faces drawn on by our elder brother.' A woman from the West Riding of Yorkshire told me in 1975 that members of her family still dye eggs at

Easter-time, using onion skins and flowers. This is a custom that prevails in many areas of England; of all Easter customs the ones involving eggs have survived longest and most children now receive the popular sweet-filled chocolate eggs as gifts on Easter Day.

In early Christian days priests were given eggs to use in church services at Easter, the eggs being consecrated and regarded as holy gifts when given to anyone. After the Reformation eggs were no longer used in church ceremonies and became more closely involved in the egg-games of the season.

Many countries preserved the tradition of egg-rolling until well into the present century and it still survives in some districts. This rolling is symbolic of the rolling away of the stone from the entrance to Christ's tomb and can be witnessed on Easter Monday afternoon in Avenham Park, Preston. Brighly decorated hard-boiled eggs are rolled down a slope and when the shells break the eggs are eaten. A woman in her early seventies, living near Carlisle, told me in 1973: 'We used to go to what they called the Milking Hill and roll our eggs down and dump them. We used to start our eggs off at the top of the hill, which wasn't very high and race them against the others. If they hadn't broken at the bottom we used to dump, or crack, each others eggs. We had them pointed end up and the other person would have a bat at it with their egg. Whichever egg cracked the most eggs, without itself breaking, was the winner. It was really just a game. Our parents dyed our eggs with onion peelings or flowers from the broom. Of course, we just ate them, but we didn't have too many. Our parents used to come and sit on the grass and watch. This was during the Easter holidays from school but I think the weather was much better then.'

There was great competition among other people to keep ones egg intact for as long as possible and the 'dumping' referred to above was known in other parts of the north as 'shackling'. In Birkenhead, eggs were rolled down those low hills known as The Bowks which now form part of Birkenhead Park. Wickets were set at the foot of the hills and it was intended that the eggs should roll between them.

Eastertime is suitably associated with many beautiful old beliefs, one being that if one should arise very early upon Easter Day and stand on some local hill, the sun will be seen to dance for joy of the Resurrection as it ascends into view. The young people who now climb nearby hills on Easter Sunday afternoon are usually unaware of any significance in their outing, but these groups are nevertheless continuing the ancient tradition. Rivington Pike, near Bolton, is the target for large crowds of young people from all over South Lancashire and, throughout the north, local peaks are traditionally sought on Easter Day.

A description is given in Carmina Gaedelica of an old Highland woman's unforgettable experience one Easter morning when 'The glorious gold-bright sun was after rising on the crests of the great hills and it was changing colour—green, purple, red, blood-red, white, intense-white and gold-white, like the glory of the God of the elements to the children of men. It was dancing up and down in exhultation at the joyous resurrection of the beloved Saviour of victory'.

Some authorities believe that the word Easter derives from the Saxon 'oster', to rise, but the Venerable Bede traced it to 'Eostre', the pagan goddess of the dawn and whose festival was held in the Spring. Spring was certainly a time for sun worship, in some parts of England there have been ceremonies since ancient times to greet the sun on some set day in Spring.

Another old conviction was that misfortune would befall anyone to go out on Easter Sunday without wearing new clothes. A new hat alone was acceptable, but the tradition became so well established in the north that many people were prevented from going to worship in church on this glorious day because they felt ashamed at not being able to afford new clothes. An elderly Cumbrian woman told me: 'I remember Easter Sunday we all got new dresses, little boys were what they called "breeched" the same day. They would perhaps have worn dresses and pinafores until they were three years old but on Easter Sunday they would visit their neighbours to show off their trousers and they always got either a few coppers in their pockets or a dyed pasche-egg.'

Together with a tradition of wearing new clothes on Easter Day comes that of spring-cleaning before-hand, and possibly these traditions were founded on a respect for the Christian faith. A sixteenth century book tells how 'This daye is called in many places, Godde's Sondaye; ye know well that it is the maner at this daye to do the fyre out of the hall, and the blacke winter brandes, and all thynges that is foule with fume and smoke shall be done awaye, and where the fyre was shall be gayly arrayed with fayre floures, and strewed with green rysshes all aboute'.

Centuries ago, Easter Eve was the time when some churches held a ceremony of making 'new fire'. The church would be in darkness when people entered, as a symbol of Christ's death on Good Friday and when His light was lost to the world. At some point during the service, flames would be lit to symbolise His resurrection.

A strange custom survived in Ashton-under-Lyne for five hundred years, when memory of the harshness and cruelty of Sir Ralph Assheton was perpetuated each Easter Monday by the townspeople. The tradition of 'Riding the Black Lad' involved a straw effigy of the knight in dragoon's helmet and cuirass. This was carried on horseback in procession around the town all afternoon before being used as target for shooting, then was burned. The day started with a fair but crowds would rush to watch the procession in the afternoon.

Some years earlier a law had been passed empowering each lord of the manor to inspect his tenant's fields for 'gulds' or corn marigolds which had been discovered to have a bad effect upon corn. This 'guld-riding' had not been enforced for some time in Ashton by the then lord of the manor, Sir John Assheton, until one Spring day when his son, Sir Ralph, together with a group of followers, rode out on inspection on his father's behalf.

He discovered that a large area of low-lying land, known as Low Carr, was over-run with the weeds and at once demanded the customary fine of a wether lamb from each tenant involved. The farmers refused since he was not their landowner, but they were imprisoned and later hanged on Gallows Field near Ashton.

The entire community afterwards lived in fear of Sir Ralph who became known as The Black Knight, and this fear was expressed in prayer.

'Sweet Jesus, for Thy mercys sake
And for The bitter passion,
Save us from the Tower axe
And from Sir Ralph Assheton'.

APRIL

The first day of April is one on which an old custom is still remembered, with many adults and certainly all children enjoying the practical jokes performed before twelve o' clock noon. After this time of day, anyone continuing to play the fool becomes the figure of fun, for then the rhyme is quoted

'April Noddy's past and gone
And you're the fool for thinking on'.

This tradition is still common in the north, as it is elsewhere, but it's origin is obscure. One explanation is that in the old calendar, April 12th and 13th (now the 1st and 2nd) were days on which the first cuckoo might be heard. Some centuries ago a common trick was to send a victim from one place to another bearing a letter which he would be invited to read himself just before noon. It contained the following rhyme, the word 'gowk' being a northern one for the cuckoo:

'The first and seconde of Aprile,
Hound the gowk another mile'.

In 'Poor Robin's Almanack' for 1760 it was stated:
'The first of April, some do say
Is set apart for All Fool's Day;
But why the people call it so
Nor I, nor they themselves do know'.

Another theory for the first of April being known as All Fool's Day was suggested in 1766 by a writer in the 'Gentleman's Magazine'. He implied that in the days when the New Year began on March 25th, the traditional week of festivities ended upon April 1st, which 'became a day of extraordinary mirth and festivity, especially among the lower sort, who are apt to pervert and to make bad use of institutions, which at first might be very laudable in themselves'.

Two weeks after Easter was the time for the annual Hock-tide Sports when, on Hock Monday, men would tie up the women they encountered, releasing them on payment of a coin as forfeit. The following day this was reversed, with woman generally raising more money than the men. This was often given to charity. A similar custom practised all over the country, and recorded in

Hartlepool early last century, was for the young men to remove the buckles from girl's shoes and only to return them in payment of a small gift. The next day the girls obeyed tradition and retaliated.

Ascension Day was unmarked by any customary observance other than church-going but in the mid-nineteenth century it was still the practice for young people to place rushes upon their doorsteps to distinguish the day. This was perhaps a surviving remnant of the tradition of strewing streets with branches and rushes before the procession passed in pre-Reformation days. The Monday, Tuesday and Wednesday before Ascension Day were known as Rogation Days, when it was customary to process round the parish boundaries and ask God's blessing on the harvest. It also became the natural time to mark out the boundaries for future generations and this custom was known as 'Beating the Bounds', which was always of secondary importance to the religious observances.

In Roman times, gods of the fields were worshipped at the Terminalia Festival and sacrifices were offered to the gods to ensure crop fertility in the festival Ambarvalia, when the fields were also perambulated. From primitive times man has always possessed this instinct to worship, an instinct which would remain forever unsatisfied without the existence of a God to worship.

Right: Girls continuing the old country custom of 'primrosing' in the Spring of 1894 at Cowling Beck in Yorkshire.

In the sixth century, Rogation Days were fixed for the blessing of fields and streams and in some rural areas the custom is still observed, but at different times of the year.

A similar ceremony is held at Norham, near Berwick-upon-Tweed, at the start of the salmon net-fishing. Held just before midnight on February 14th, this open-air service ends in time for the boat to get out as midnight strikes. If the first net brings in a salmon this is ceremoniously given to the vicar. Participants in the service are asked to take torches and if the 14th or 15th of February falls on a Sunday then the Blessing is postponed until 6 a.m. on Monday.

Cullercoats and North Shields are among the towns and villages where boats have been ceremoniously blessed, while it was common practice in past days to hold services to bless the source of water, whether from well or spring.

George Herbert wrote in the early seventeenth century: 'The country parson is a lover of old customs, if they be good and harmless. Particularly he loves procession and maintains it, because there are contained in it four manifest advantages. 1. A blessing of God for the fruits of the earth. 2. Justice in the preservation of bounds. 3. Charity, in loving, walking and neighbourly accompanying one another, with reconciling of differences at that time, if there be any. 4. Mercy, in relieving the poor by a liberal distribution and largess, which at that time, is or ought to be, used'.

Beating the Bounds is frequently held in the autumn but takes place at Morpeth on the Thursday nearest St. Marks Day, April 25th, although no longer held annually. The boundary riding in Morpeth is done on horseback, starting at noon and taking the entire afternoon.

Berwick-upon-Tweed can, with its annual ceremony of Riding the Bounds, boast a tradition which has continued unbroken since the reign of Henry VIII. Again on horseback, the boundary-marking begins at 11 a.m. each May 1st., unless this falls on a Sunday when it is held on the 2nd, the Mayor and civic dignitaries following the party of horseman in a coach.

Also held in May is the Newbiggin-by-the-Sea ceremony of Riding the Bounds, while Lancaster continues the custom in June, but not annually.

A unique Ascension-tide rite is performed each year in Whitby when, at 9 a.m. (tides permitting), the Penny Hedge is planted on the east bank of the Esk. This Ascension-Eve ritual commemorates the forgiveness of a twelfth century monk from Whitby Abbey who lived a life of prayer and meditation in a small chapel in the woods of Eskdale. One day he gave refuge to a wild boar which was being pursued by a party of huntsmen including William de Bruce and Ralph de Piercie. The hunters had angrily set their hounds upon the monk then had fled in terror to Scarborough, leaving him mortally wounded. The Abbot of Whitby happened to be a friend of the King's and he was granted royal permission to exert the full penalty—death. The hermit heard of this and just before his death granted his murderers forgiveness, as Christ Himself had done before His death upon the cross. At the same time, the hermit gave them a charge that they and their successors must, each year until the end of time, plant a hedge on Ascension Eve as penance for their souls. If they failed to do this their property would be handed to Whitby Abbey.

To complete the rite in its entirety, a representative for the family must enter the wood at sunrise to receive ten strong props or 'stowers' from an officer of the Abbey, ten 'yedders', which are supple branches, and ten staves. These are carried to the water's edge where the token hedge is erected and must fulfil the condition of standing through three tides 'without removing by the Force of Water'. As the last stick is driven in, a bailiff blows his horn while another cries out three times 'Out on you'.

MAY

The month of May has been, since early times, the season for merrymaking. After James I was petitioned by the people of Lancashire for a return to favour of the dancing, church-ales and other recreation previously customary on Sunday after church-going, he had published the 'Book of Sports'. In this he gave permission for, and encouraged the return of, Sunday pastimes. The book expressed the King's wish that 'for his good people's lawful recreation, after the end of Divine service, that his good people be not disturbed, or discouraged, from any lawful recreation, such as dancing for men and women, archery for men, leaping, vaulting, or any such harmless recreations; nor from having May games, Whitsun ales, and morris dances, and the setting up of May-poles, and other sports therewith used, so as the same be had in due and convenient time, without impediment or neglect of Divine service'.

Since the Second World War, the holding of 'May Queens', a popular custom of town and country life, has greatly declined but larger combined May Festivals are held in many counties. The Gawthorpe Feast is held annually on the first Saturday in May near Ossett, with a May Queen and maids of honour on horseback in procession with other riders, a band, decorated vehicles and all the colour and excitement expected of a north-country celebration. The festive day ends with displays of Maypole dancing.

Right: A photograph taken in 1907 of the Stockport May Fair, with typical stalls of the period selling ice-cream and probably hot peas. May-time festivities have been held for thousands of years, originally to celebrate the arrival of Spring. Early celebrations would involve the propitiation of the pagan gods of fields, plants and trees as well as being pleas for continued fertility of crops, animals and man. Last century, much of the folk-dancing, games and racing began to die out and be replaced by fun-fairs which were characterised by roundabouts, coconut-shies, food-stalls and side shows of all kinds.

A similar ceremony takes place in Knutsford on the first Saturday of May each year, and other small northern towns and villages also hold May-time celebrations. The comparatively simple, combined efforts of families from small areas in a town do appear to have died out. These were planned from Easter onwards, with parents perhaps assisting and certainly promising a contribution towards the tea.

A Manchester man told me in 1974: 'There was the Queen with a train of probably their mother's old curtains, flowers in her hair and a paper crown, the train-bearers, the butcher, the baker, the miner with his black face and pick and spade and of course the girl with the collecting box going from door to door. They used to sing at every house. Some had a Maypole as well and danced round the Maypole. Now all this has gone out.'

The little procession of children wound its way around the streets and could see other groups of children in their 'May Queen'. One woman said: 'There was a good bit of rivalry over who had the best turn-out. I was in terrible disgrace once with my mother because we had all been invited inside a public-house to sing. I must say, we got the best collection ever that day and the best telling-off from my mother.'

The money collected was sometimes shared among the children taking part, sometimes went to charity but often went to buy 'lemonade and biscuits', as a Cumbrian woman described. She explained: 'When May Day came around we used to gather wild flowers in the wood and make crowns or decorate hoops. We begged old lace curtains from our parents and made a train for the Queen and put on her a crown of flowers and then dressed as many children as possible with flowers and then had a procession. We called it a May Festival. We collected pennies from the houses and finished up buying lemonade and biscuits. We thought it was grand.'

Often, provision for a meal for the children on their return from processing the streets had been planned by the mothers some time before and tables would be erected in the street or a convenient garden. A Northwich woman described May Queen celebrations of her childhood to me, adding: 'There were no cars then. What a great day it used to be.'

Although the tradition varied slightly from one area to another, the basic theme was the same; for children to celebrate the coming of May with a procession and either singing or dancing somewhere along the route. Thirty years ago the singing in procession had died out but children still walked around the streets dressed as the character of their choice. As one person said: 'The Queen wore a lace curtain on her head and a long white dress belonging to an elder sister or even her mother.

One of the boys usually dressed as a baker with a white apron and a flour bag on his head—one that had previously held a dozen of flour. One girl might be a nurse dressed in white apron with a red cross stitched onto it and a white hankie on her head. Any old dressing-up clothes were used but at least we knew the words of our song.' She was speaking of the period from 1905 until the start of the First World War. Singing of course died out after this time; probably, as with many traditions, the influence of the war brought about a gradual decline in singing the old May songs. Many elderly people are proud of the quality of their singing, one woman from Durham telling me that she and her friends 'practised our May songs for weeks before', and a variety of songs has been quoted to me, both those used by the children in their May Queen processions and those sung in schools.

In mediaeval days every village would have a maypole to dance around on May Day, but the Puritans disapproved the pagan rite. In 1644 the Long Parliament ordered that all maypoles must be taken down. The primitive custom, which had originated many centuries earlier, ceased until after the Reformation. Dancing around the maypole was considered by the Romans and Saxons to be an appeal to the pagan gods for fertility; originally the 'pole' would be a tree but eventually wooden posts were substituted as being more expedient. When it was again possible for maypoles to be set up they were sometimes kept as a permanent fixture on the village green, but others were taken down and stored after the annual festivities. Maypoles can still be seen at Temple Sowerby and at Barwick in Elmet, the latter is said to be the oldest in England. At Barwick in Elmet a May Festival is held every three years, then the pole is taken down to be repainted and will be decked with flowers and ribbons before the next Maytime dancing. This is of the type which has come to be closely associated with maypoles, but before the revival in the 1880's of Maytime festivities the dancing was much more robust, noisy and lusty.

Until the coming of railways ousted the horse and coach from its previously unrivalled position of importance, May Day frequently saw the parade of horses and vehicles from coaching houses. Their importance in transport was celebrated in a procession including all types of horse-drawn vehicles, with the horses wearing new harness which was often decorated with posies of flowers. Manchester was one place holding a large procession on May Day and people flocked to it from miles around to see the huge draught horses, with plaited manes and tails, dressed with coloured ribbons, and others pulling coaches from the numerous coaching houses in the city.

A man from County Durham told me in 1975: 'I started school when I was five in 1910 at South Shields and shortly afterwards received a Coronation mug at King George's coronation. In those days and during the 1914-18 War, all the horses on horse-driven vehicles—there were milk carts, coal carts, grocery carts and just about every kind of cart, were all decorated with plumes, ribbons, rosettes and flowers every May Day, and nearly all the vehicles were horse-drawn then, there were very few motor cars or motor vehicles. As my birthday was May first I took great pleasure in seeing all the horses so nicely decorated.'

In the same era, the 'Mayers' had 'sung in' the month of May in customary fashion. This was common custom in Swinton, near Manchester, where four to six men with a few musical instruments (and always a fiddle) sang one of the May Songs around the town from the beginning or middle of April until the last night of the month, to 'sing-in' the month of May. This custom probably originated in pagan times with the superstitious belief that the singing of May songs would dispel the gloom of winter.

The oldest recorded May song begins:
'All in this pleasant evening together come we,
For the summer springs so fresh, green and gay;
We'll tell you of a blossom that buds on every tree,
Drawing near to the merry month of May.'

and after calling upon all members of the household to 'rise up' the song offers God's blessing to them all, to conclude:

'So now we're going to leave you in peace and plenty here,
For the summer springs so fresh, green and gay.
We shall not sing you May again until another year,
For to draw these cold winters away.'

The last line recalls the superstition of 'drawing away' or dispelling the winter with the singing.

Another, less ancient, song sung in the Manchester area long ago is said to have been written by a Swinton man and called 'The Basiers' after the auricula, a flower in bloom in April. Auricula, when introduced into this country in 1567 from Switzerland, was known as bear's ears from the shape of it's leaf and the Lancashire pronunciation of this altered it to 'basiers'.

New May Song

'When the trees are in bloom, and the meadows are green,
The sweet-smelling cowslips are plain to be seen,
The sweet ties of nature, which plainly do say,
For the basiers are sweet in the morning of May.

All creatures are deemed, in their station below
Such comforts of love on each other bestow;
Our flocks they're all folded and young lambs sweetly do play,
And the basiers are sweet in the morning of May.

So now to conclude with much freedom and love,
The sweetest of blessings proceeds from above;
Let us join in our song, that right happy may we be,
For we're blest with content in the morning of May'.

Many elderly people in South Lancashire gave me the words of the following song which they remembered singing as children in their May Queen processions:

'May Day, May Day, bright and gay day,
Gone the month of April showers.
The Queen of May is here today
To give you all a holiday.
Hail, all hail, the merry, merry month of May,
We'll hasten to the woods away and we shall be so
bright and gay,
So hail, all hail, the merry, merry month of May.
We bring you sweet posies,
Lilies and roses,
Ladies, who'll buy? Ladies, who'll buy'?

This was also described to me by a woman from Blackburn as the most popular May song in her district when she was a child.

A May song popular in Yorkshire at the turn of the century began:
'T'was on the morn of sweet May Day,
When nature painted all things gay.'

Right: A choir outing, photographed at High Force in 1912, with best hats and buttoned boots to the fore. Such outings were eagerly anticipated from one year to the next and the picnic-tea often provided the highlight of the day, which was often the only one on which a family might have opportunity to go on a country outing. Children were also catered for, with Field Days or Sunday School excursions. These combined a short trip out into the countryside with sports, games and the picnic-tea.

and the song concludes:

'Young Jockey early in the morn
Arose, and tripped it o'er the lawn,
His Sunday coat, the youth put on
For Jennie had vowed away to run
With Jockey to the fair'

A May Day custom peculiar to Yorkshire was that of 'May Gesling', when a second Fool's Day was practised as on April 1st, with all the mischief that the young people and older were capable of undertaking. May Gesling is remembered as occurring well into this century but again World War II seemed to hasten its decline in popularity. Sometimes known as 'May Gosling' the name of this Fool's day probably derives from the foolish, goose-like behaviour of most people on this day, but there is no apparent source for the custom.

Field Days began last century and continued until the 1940s when it was customary to take all the Sunday School classes on an afternoon outing to enjoy a small picnic and to play games. Most people remember these with great enjoyment as being one of the rare days when whole families spent an afternoon in the countryside and away from crowded towns. Even those already living in the lovely rural areas of the north looked forward eagerly to the Field Day when they might be taken for a ride in a charabanc, then take part in the games and sports after tea. One woman, however, whose father had owned his own pony and trap perhaps felt that a picnic was a common enough event for she told me: 'I was only once taken on a Field Day, which was a Sunday School outing. We were herded onto flat lorries and a fence put round us. We each had to take a mug which had to be tied on to us in some way. We each had a very large bun and a cake and there were sports, for which I was too young to enter.'

The Leyland May Festival was an event originally organised by Sunday School teachers. It was intended to hold a children's fete then to crown the girl selected as May Queen and the custom was initiated on May 29th 1889. The affair became so popular, including as it did Morris Dancers and other entertainments, that it became an annual event.

May 29th was also commonly known as Oak Apple Day when bunches of oak leaves were hung outside public houses and children invariably wore a spring of oak leaves to school. Many people in all counties of the north still remember the 'fun' on Oak Apple Day and have described to me the similar activities of children in all counties on that day when: 'If we arrived at school without an oak leaf we were nettled by the other children. And if you haven't been stung with a nettle you won't know how painful it is.' (Cheshire.)

'We had a public house in Little Hulton called "The Royal Oak", and I remember seeing bunches of oak leaves tied there on Royal Oak Day.'

'I distinctly remember the little rhyme we used to recite to one another as school-children in nineteen-ten or earlier,

"Twenty-ninth of May,

Royal Oak Day.
If you don't give us a holiday
We'll all run away."

This rhyme would crop up every year in May. It never seemed to have any effect on the authorities, we never said it to them, only to ourselves. There was never any holiday on Royal Oak Day'. (Yorkshire.)

This custom marks Restoration Day. On May 29th, 1660, King Charles II celebrated his return to the throne of England with a triumphant entry into London. An Act of Parliament declared the day one of national thanksgiving, and until 1859 it was a public holiday. The earing of oak leaves commemorates the King's escape after the Battle of Worcester, when he hid from his pursuers in an oak tree at Boscobel. Charles II founded the Royal Hospital, Chelsea, now the home of the Chelsea Pensioners, and each year on Restoration Day the King's statue is decorated with oak leaves.

Right: A photograph of a 'May Queen', circa 1919. The children were obviously proud of their pretty dresses and enormous hair ribbons The broom-handle May-pole had been decorated with coloured ribbons by the mother of one of the children. This photograph was lent by the sister of the girl who was May Queen for the day. She said: 'And my sister is carrying a basket and has a lace curtain on her head. She is enclosed in a decorated hoop with her lady-in-waiting. We always had little baskets full of flowers on Walking Day and at Whitsuntide'.

At Tonge Fold, near Bolton, a beautifully carved wooden figure representing King Charles was kept in the house of the oldest inhabitant. It was brought out by the villagers on the Sunday before May 29th and carried in procession along Bury Road to Bradshawgate and back, accompanied by Morris Dancers. On the morning of 'Oak Apple Day' the figure was tied to an oak tree at the 'Dog and Kennel' inn, then taken into the tap-room in the evening. The 'nomination verses' or 'Nominy', composed about 1848, were then read aloud and pints of beer drunk in honour of the figure.

The image of King Charles remained in the inn for a week where mothers brought children to kiss him and flowers were placed in his hand, then he was returned to the home of the village ancient.

May was one of the customary times for the hiring of new employees, the other being Martinmas, and the event brought great activity to many towns all over the country. Although the Hiring Fairs died out early this century, the north remains the home of great annual meetings with the Brough Hill Fair at Appleby being one of the most important. In 1685 James II granted a charter for the 'purchase and sale of all manner of goods, cattle, horses, mares and geldings' at Appleby, but now only horses are traded here, with more than half the gipsies in the country converging on the town. Farmers flock to the fair to buy horses but the gipsies rarely trade among themselves while here. Spontaneous demonstrations of excellent horsemanship are witnessed by the crowds of people along Boroughgate where shop fronts are temporarily boarded. The fair is a unique event, probably the only one of its kind to survive.

A newspaper article early this century described 'the great annual horse, cattle and sheep fair known as Brough Hill', going on to say 'For weeks potter's carts, smart gipsy vans, and nondescript equipages of all sorts have been gradually moving from all parts of the compass to this part of Westmorland, with which almost every horse and cattle dealer in the three kingdoms is familiar'. Cattle were still a feature of the fair although the writer explained 'Herds of beautiful long-horned Highland cattle, numbering thousands, used to be a feature of this fair, but rarely more than two or three hundred are now shown'.

Another custom observed on May 29th is the Commemoration of the Battle of Neville's Cross held in Durham Cathedral. On October 17th, 1346, monks chanted prayers from the Cathedral tower as they watched the battle. The abbot promised that each year prayers of thanksgiving would be offered from the same spot if God offered His help to quell the Scottish invaders. When a messenger brought news of the capture of the Scottish leader and defeat of his forces the monks raised up a joyous Te Deum. The custom was discontinued during the Civil War but was later revived and held on May 29th in honour of the Restoration. Bach year the Cathedral choir ascends the west tower after Evensong to sing three anthems; one is sung from each side of the tower but never the west side, since tradition has it that from here a choir boy once fell to his death.

JUNE

Whitsuntide comes seven weeks after Easter and its customs all celebrate the fulfillment of Christ's words 'I am with you always, to the close of the age', for on the first Whit Sunday the Holy Spirit came to Christians for the first time to give His power and support for their work as disciples.

From very early times Whitsuntide was devoted to festivities, ranging from sports and Morris Dances to Miracle and Mystery Plays. The most famous of these plays were performed at Chester and at York, often depicting the story of creation. Each guild in the town or city chose a particular play, combining to present the whole. In 1600 twenty-five guilds in Chester presented the entire story of man from his creation to the last judgement. The Drapers performed the story of creation, the Barbers the story of Abraham and Isaac, and so on.

Miracle Plays generally depicted stories from the Old Testament while the Mystery Plays told of the life of Christ, concentrating upon the New Testament. Both Miracle and Mystery Plays are sometimes performed in York and in Chester, usually as part of a major festival. The setting is now static, whereas in mediaeval days each cycle of plays would be presented from an enormous wheeled cart which could be moved from one part of the town to another.

The beautiful, symbolic dramas were watched with great respect and reverence by audiences familiar with the stories but who very much enjoyed seeing them dramatised. On the other hand, any amusing incident was extended by the actors and enlivened by shouts of laughter and cat-calls from the audience. The sincere but lively acting and boisterous humour of the audience were typical of the mediaeval period, unfortunately during the Victorian era solemnity in one's worship was carried to the extreme of believing it virtuous to regard all aspects of Christianity as humourless and joyless.

Whit Sunday has traditionally been the time for processions of witness all over the north of England for many years. The day also marked the start of a short holiday for those who were overworked in the industrial towns of the nineteenth century. During Whit week 1848, approximately 116,000 people took advantage of the cheap train excursions, and two years later the figure had risen to 202,500.

Right: 'Walking Day' and Whitsuntide processions have been important features of community life for many years, with villages combining in walks of witness. Until the 19th century, 'Church Ales' gave people opportunity to give aid to the needy but these died out, Club Walks developing and taking their place. These in time became the 'Walking Days' familiar throughout the north of England.

The photograph showing a Whit Friday procession on Clover Street, Rochdale, was taken in 1905.

The annual Whit Walks in Manchester, begun in 1801, had a deep religious significance and while, after the Second World War, the walks had tended to become processions for the display of new garments rather than of witness to faith, it is probably true to say that, although numbers have now decreased, those participating are once again doing so as a mark of their faith. A Northumbrian woman said to me: 'We still have our Whit-tide walks of witness and now instead of each church walking separately we seem to unite more, which to my mind is good.'

Some experts think that the name for this season derives from the word 'white' since those baptised on Whit Sunday wore white garments. Another opinion is that it refers to the custom of the rich giving all the milk from their cows to the poor on Whit Sunday. The Old English words 'Hwita Sunnandaeg' were given to the day many centuries ago and they mean White Sunday, a reference to the robes worn by the newly baptised at Pentecost.

In the fourteenth century a verse was written to suggest that the word Whit means 'wit' or 'wisdom', a reference to the miraculous gifts bestowed upon Christ's disciples on Pentecost.

'This day Whitsunday is cald,
For wisdom and wit sevenfold
Was goven to the Apostles on this day'.

It was traditional in Lancashire to bake a special type of cake to eat on Whit Sunday, a yeast confection rather like a muffin with sugar on top. Almost every county has it's own Whitsuntide specialities, Durham and Yorkshire being renowned for delicious cheesecakes traditionally served on Whitsunday. Whitsun was also at one time the season particularly devoted to Morris Dancing, especially in the sixteenth and seventeenth centuries, but the dances later became more closely associated with Easter.

Until the end of the nineteenth century, Church-Ales were a regular occurrence in a community, being held three or four times a year and always at Whitsuntide. They served to raise money for church funds or to be passed on to any poor or destitute family or person in the parish. The church wardens either bought, or were given, gifts of malt which they brewed to sell on the given day in the church house. Everyone in the parish was expected to attend or to pay a fine and during the evening there would be the usual singing and dancing with ballad singers and Morris Dancers sometimes coming to entertain. One writer of the 1870's wrote: 'In every parish was a church house, to which belonged spits, crocks and other utensils for dressing provisions. Here the housekeepers met. The young people were there, too, and had dancing, bowling, shooting at butts etc., the ancients sitting gravely by and looking on. All things were civil and without scandal. The church ale is, doubtless, derived from the Agapai or Love Feasts, mentioned in the New Testament'.

Right: Another Whit Friday procession; St. Anne's at Brindle Heath in 1908.

As with many of our customs which drew a community together the Church-Ale has long been a thing of the past.

St. John's Day, on June 24th, is also Midsummer Day. On the eve of this day the ancients lit fires on hill-tops, leaping through the flames and burning bones to ward off evil spirits. Closely associated with Druidical rites, these bonfires were also known in Roman days and in other countries. In Scandinavia they were dedicated to the gods Thor and Odin.

Even now the heathen believe that on Midsummer Eve the mystic force linking heaven and earth is strongest and strange pagan ceremonies take place. Throughout Europe, the custom for lighting bonfires on this night survived for centuries although they later became dedicated to St. John. In the ninth century, however, Charlemagne forbad the custom as being of pagan origin.

Flowers and birch branches were used to decorate houses and churches on St. John's Day, the most widely used being roses, lilies, and St. John's Wort, this latter supposed to ward off evil.

On St. John's Eve a popular custom in some areas of the north was for young men to go out gathering the seed of ferns. These would be used to attract the attention of a girl they admired but who would not return their affection. The seeds, or spores, of ferns were given many strange attributes, including a protection aginst witches and demons but their power was believed to be so great that the evil ones made it extremely difficult for anyone to collect them on St. John's Eve. Shakespeare wrote in Henry IV, Act 2, Scene 1: 'I think you are more beholding to the night than to fern seed for your walking invisible'.

The seed was also accredited with powers of divination and it was believed to be possible to see its custodian, the Queen of the Fairies, at this time of the year only.